A NEW WAY
of LIVING

A NEW WAY of LIVING

Understanding What It Means to Accept Christ

JOYCE MEYER

New York   Boston   Nashville

FaithWords

Hachette Book Group
237 Park Avenue, New York, NY 10017
Visit our Web site at www.faithwords.com.

FaithWords and the FaithWords logo are trademarks of
Hachette Book Group

The author would like to acknowledge that the story used in chapter 3,
on pages 11–13, is an original sermon illustration by Dr. Monroe Parker
and is used by permission of Gospel Projects Press, P.O. Box 643,
Milton, FL 32572; copyright 1977. www.childrensbibleclub.com

Printed in the United States of America

First Edition: December 2006

10 9 8 7 6

Library of Congress Cataloging-in-Publication Data
Meyer, Joyce
A new way of living : understanding what it means to
accept Christ / Joyce Meyer.—1st ed.
    p.   cm.
ISBN 978-0-446-58155-4
1. Christian life.   I. Title.
BV4501.3.M492 2006
248.4—dc22   2006031877

CONTENTS

Chapter 1

THE MOST IMPORTANT DECISION YOU WILL EVER MAKE

Are you dissatisfied with your life? If so, you are not alone. Multitudes of people are tired, weary, empty, and unfulfilled. Some have tried religion in hopes of finding a solution to the way they feel, only to be burdened with lifeless and unreasonable rules that they couldn't keep. If you have tried religion, it does not mean you've tried God as the solution to your empty, frustrating, guilt-ridden life.

If you need to feel loved, if you need a friend, if you need your sins forgiven, and if you need a future...Jesus Christ is your answer. He is waiting to give you a new life and make you a brand new creation.

If you are not satisfied with your life, you must change something. If we keep doing the same things we have always done, we will have the life we have always had. You need to make a decision, and it is the most important decision you will ever make.

This decision is more important than your career choice, where you will attend college, whom you will marry, how you will invest your money, or where you will live. This decision concerns eternity. Eternity is time without end, and each of us needs to know where we will spend it. There is life after death. When you die, you don't cease to exist, you just begin to exist in another place. It has been said that dying is like going through a revolving door. You simply leave one place and go to another.

Do you want to have a relationship with God here on earth and live with Him for eternity? If so, you need to receive Jesus Christ as your Savior. We have all sinned and we all need a Savior. God sent His only Son to pay the penalty for our sins. He was crucified and shed His innocent blood as payment for our wrongdoing. He died and was buried, but on the third day He rose from the dead and is now seated in heaven, at the right hand of God the Father. He is your only hope of having peace, joy and right standing with God.

In order to be saved from our sins, the Bible teaches that we must confess and acknowledge that Jesus is Lord, and we must believe in our hearts that God raised Him from the dead.

Because if you acknowledge *and* confess with your lips that Jesus is Lord and in your heart believe (adhere to, trust in, and rely on the truth) that God raised Him from the dead, you will be saved. —ROMANS 10:9

This type of believing is more than a mental acknowledgement, it is sincere and heartfelt. Many people believe there is a God, but they have not committed their lives to Him. God is the Author of Life, and He wants you to willingly and gladly give your life back to Him. God created you with a free will and He will not force you to choose Him. But whether you do or not will make the difference in the quality of life you live while here on earth, and it is the deciding factor in where you will spend eternity when you die.

Have you done a good job of running your life? If not, why not turn it over to the One who created you and knows more about you than you will ever know about yourself? If I buy an automobile and start having trouble with it, I take it back to the people who manufactured it so they can fix it. It is the same principle with God. He created you and loves you very much. If your life is not satisfying to you then take it to Him so He can fix it.

As I said previously, nothing changes unless you make a decision. Do you want to be a Christian? Are you ready to surrender not only your sin to God but your life as well? Are you ready to turn from your sinful ways and learn how to live a brand new life that is lived with and for God? If so, keep reading because there is a life waiting for you beyond the best thing you could possibly imagine. It is available to all. No one is left out. This is what God says about your future:

For I know the thoughts *and* plans that I have for you, says the Lord, thoughts *and* plans for welfare and peace *and* not for evil, to give you hope in your final outcome.

—JEREMIAH 29:11

No one can make your choice for you. It is yours and yours alone to make. What quality of life do you desire to have? Do you really want to follow the example you see in our society today? God's Word says we came into the world with nothing and we will go out with nothing (1 Timothy 6:7). God is the Alpha and the Omega, the beginning and the end. In the beginning there was God, and in the end there will be God. Every person will stand before God and give an account of their life (Romans 14:12). Now is the time to get ready for that. I always say, "Ready or not, Jesus is coming." Get ready now, make the right decision now, because later may be too late.

Chapter 2

WE HAVE ALL SINNED

❧Sin is deliberate disobedience to the known will of God. We have all sinned. There is no one on the earth who never sins (Romans 3:23, Ecclesiastes 7:20). That's the bad news, but there is also good news. We can all be forgiven and made right with God.

> Since all have sinned and are falling short of the honor *and* glory which God bestows *and* receives.
> [All] are justified *and* made upright *and* in right standing with God, freely *and* gratuitously by His grace (His unmerited favor and mercy) through the redemption which is [provided] in Christ Jesus.
> —ROMANS 3:23–24

Jesus has already paid for your sins; all you need to do is believe it and receive it. If you will admit your sins, be sorry for them and be willing to turn entirely away from them, God will forgive you and make you a new person.

> If we [freely] admit that we have sinned *and* confess our sins, He is faithful and just (true to His own nature and promises) and will forgive our sins [dismiss our lawlessness] and [continuously] cleanse us from all unrighteousness [everything not in conformity to His will in purpose, thought, and action]. —1 JOHN 1:9

You need not wait on God to do something. He has already done what needs to be done. He gave His only Son to die in our place because only a perfect and sinless sacrifice could be offered to pay for our misdeeds. Justice has been satisfied, and we can go free through believing in Jesus Christ and by entering an intimate relationship with God through Him. We cannot go to God on our own—we need an advocate. We need someone as a go-between, and that someone is Jesus. Jesus stood in the gap between us and God, the gap that our sin created, and He brings us to God.

Just as a child has his father in him (his blood, his DNA, chromosomes, etc.), so God was in Christ reconciling the world back to Himself. God loves the people He created, and He is unwilling to see them sold into the slavery of sin without providing a way out. Jesus is the way!